Count Us In ✔

Writers: David Dalziel, Judy Jarvis, David Morgan, Anthony Reddie and Elaine Robinson
Adviser: Ruth Yeoman
Editors: Elizabeth Bruce and Judy Jarvis

Published by:
National Christian Education Council
1020 Bristol Road
Selly Oak
Birmingham
B29 6LB

British Cataloguing-in-Publication Data:
A catalogue record for this book is available from the British Library.

ISBN 0-7197-0919-9

Designed and typeset by Liam Purcell, National Christian Education Council.
Printed and bound by Ebenezer Baylis, Worcester

CONTENTS

The editors and publishers gratefully acknowledge permission to reproduce the following material, but if any rights have inadvertently been overlooked, the necessary correction will gladly be made in subsequent editions.

''Caring, sharing' by Linda Caroe from *Big Blue Planet*, published by Stainer & Bell and the Methodist Church Division of Education & Youth, 1995. Used by permission of Lianda Caroe.

'Contact' by Donald Hilton from *Flowing Streams*, published by National Christian Education Council, 1993. Used by permission of Donald Hilton.

'Halle, halle, halle' from *Many and Great,* published by Wild Goose. Permission sought.

'I may not have...' by David Jenkins from *The Word in the World*, published by National Christian Education Council, 1997. Permission sought.

'Letter to an erstwhile prodigal son' by Geoffrey King from the Methodist Recorder, 5 March 1998. Used by permission of Geoffrey King.

'Life is great!' by Brian A Wren from *Rejoice and Sing*, published by Oxford University Press, 1991. Permission sought.

'Lord, as we worship today' from the MAYC London Weekend Worship. Used by permission of MAYC.

'Lord Jesus Christ...' by Donald Hilton from *The Word in the World*, published by National Christian Education Council, 1997. Permission sought.

'May our church exist...' by Simon Oxley from *The Word in the World*, published by National Christian Education Council, 1997. Used by permission of Simon Oxley.

'The Servant Song' by Richard Gillard from *Rejoice and Sing,* published by Oxford University Press, 1991. Used by permission of Kingsway's Thankyou Music.

'Take this moment' from *Love from Below*, published by Wild Goose. Permission sought.

'We see ourselves, O God' from *Risking Obedience*, Prayer Handbook of the Uniting Church Australia. Permission sought.

Introduction

Count us in ✔

Everybody worships. Some do it at Wembley at the Cup Final. Some worship at a pop concert given by their favourite group, some in school assembly, others on a lonely mountain top. And, of course, some do it in church. Recent thinking is that it is important that people of all ages and a wide range of backgrounds have the opportunity to come together to worship. When people worship together they are united by a common focus, a common aim and the need to celebrate. For Christians there is what we might call the X factor - God is with us. *Count us in* has been written to help us celebrate God's presence with us in everything we do together.

Why Count us in?

Too often, worship in church is seen as an end in itself, isolated from the life and needs of the local community. In fact, it is vital that worship arises out of the daily experience of the whole community. *Count us in* has been written to help your church discover what it means to be an all-age worshipping community. We hope that it will be for you a starting point for further sharing as an all-age community, both in worship and in fellowship.

Aims of Count us in

Count us in is a resource to help people of all ages to discover:

✓ more about themselves;
✓ more about their relationships with each other as a community of faith;
✓ what they can learn from each other;
✓ shared experiences of awe and wonder, joy and sadness;
✓ what it means to prepare and share worship together;
✓ ways of responding together to God's love.

Beginning Count us in ✔

What is Count us in ?

Count us in is activity-based material for the whole church. You can use it as part of a regular programme of worship and learning or as an opportunity to do something completely different. It is suitable for all churches whether big or small, urban or rural. It is based on four sessions, each linking the theme of the session with a Bible story. It is no coincidence that all the Bible readings which are used for *Count us in* are concerned with food and hospitality. All great celebrations where people of all ages come together, such as wedding breakfasts, Christmas dinner, parties and Holy Communion, have food as the focus. Sharing food is a way of getting alongside each other and spending time together.

How does Count us in work?

Count us in begins with the individual, helping everyone, whatever their age or circumstances, to discover that they are valued and have a contribution to make. It then helps you to explore what it is like to be part of a community. As a community, you will discover ways of worshipping God together before preparing for and celebrating worship.

Count us in contains a great deal more material than you will need. It has been written to enable you to pick and mix from the activities within each session. Adapt them to suit your own situation. It is essential, however, that you use the sessions in the order in which they are printed.

Who is Count us in for?

Involve the whole church or as many as will come. The more people who are involved, the more people will 'own' what is happening. Remember, in some activities children and young people will have the greatest skills and expertise; in others the reverse will be true.

When can Count us in be used?

You can use *Count us in* during the week, on Sundays, for church away-days, church family weekends, or celebration weekends. It can be used over a short period of time or spread over a year. How can you get started?

As with any new venture you will need to give yourselves plenty of time to plan. Establish a planning group with representatives from different areas of your church's life. Invite other people to be responsible for individual activities within the sessions.

How can your church be counted in?

Use *Count us in* to explore together the life and worship of your church community. It contains many ideas. Choose those which are most suitable for your own situation and allow them to spark off other ideas. Only you know what is best in your particular context.

Build up a record of your church's experience of *Count us in.* Take photographs, make a video, gather together things that are produced in the sessions and use them to share what you have done with the rest of your church.

Remember....

✓ There is too much material here! Choose what you need for your particular situation.

✓ In your community people will vary in ability, experience and confidence as well as in age. Try to make it easy for everyone to contribute if they want to. You will become aware of gifts which were previously hidden. You may also discover problems of which you knew nothing.

✓ People have different pastoral needs and require different kinds of support. There may be things which need to be followed up later.

✓ Be aware of the need to respect people's confidences.

✓ Some people need to be given the opportunity to express themselves in ways other than writing. Some may have problems in hearing everything which goes on. Some may prefer to be passive while others will enjoy being very active. Try to be sensitive to the needs of everybody.

✓ You must observe good practice in all areas of health and safety.

✓ Listen to what everyone has to say. Value and respect each other's views.

✓ Have fun!

Theme	Scripture	Sessions
Finding me	Luke 19.1-10: The story of Zacchaeus	**First session:** an informal introduction to the themes (needs at least two hours) **Second session:** a framework for worship and learning for all ages
Joining in	Acts 2.42-47: The story of the first Christian community	**First session:** an informal exploration of what it means to be a community (needs at least two hours) **Second session:** a framework for worship and learning for all ages
We're in it together, God	John 6.1-13: The story of the feeding of the five thousand	**One session:** a framework for preparing and joining in worship for all ages
Stand up and be counted	Luke 15.11-32: The story of the lost son	**Preparation:** suggestions for preparing worship for all ages (needs at least two hours) **Final celebration:** over to you!

Finding Me

We are all different, with a great variety of gifts and skills. Sometimes these gifts and skills go un-recognized, both by ourselves and by other people. These are what we explore in this first part of *Count us in.*

This part will help you and your group to explore

✓   what you enjoy and what you dislike;

✓   your strengths and weaknesses.

It will help you to discover

✓   more about yourselves;

✓   how you affect other people;

✓   how they affect you.

Using the story of Zacchaeus, you will find out

✓   that Jesus cared about individuals, whoever they were;

✓   that God cares for us, whoever we are.

The grid overleaf gives you an overview of the two sessions of *Finding Me*. Detailed instructions are on the pages which follow.

Use the first session as an opportunity to get to know each other better.

Use the second session as a framework for an act of worship. The activities suggested can also be used at other times.

Finding me: FIRST SESSION

Doing	Reflecting	Going Further
Choose from: *What I can do* *Finding out* *Generation game* *Talent show*	**Choose from:** *Who do you know?* *Learning about each other* *Labelling each other* *Paper chain* *Song, reading and prayer*	**Choose from:** *Sharing skills* *Eating a meal* *Taking photographs*

Finding me: SECOND SESSION

Gathering	Doing and Reflecting	Responding
Call to worship *Hymn or song* *Prayers* *Reading: Luke 19.1-10*	*All together in one place* **Choose from:** *Who is this?* *Who am I?* *Desert island discs* *Mixed-age groups* **Choose from:** *Making our mark* *Small is clever?* *My secret file* *What do I see?* *Concentric circles*	*Sharing* *The Peace* *Song* *Prayers*

Finding me: First session

Doing

Use some of these ideas to help people of all ages to explore their individuality. The activities take very different amounts of time, so choose what best suits your situation.

What I can do

Ask people to bring photographs of themselves and also some evidence of something they are good at, for example a piece of craft work or a swimming certificate. Number the photographs and give a letter to each skill. Ask people to try to match the two (e.g. a picture of Sarah Jackson, numbered 16, should be linked with her swimming certificate marked B).

Finding out

Use the questionnaire on page 38 or make up your own. Give a copy to everyone. The challenge is to gather a signature (or, for young children, a mark) in each box. If possible all the signatures should be different.

Generation game

Choose an activity which can be demonstrated by an expert (for instance Scottish country dancing, playing a trumpet, making pastry). Organize a 'Generation game' activity, encouraging other people to have a go.

Talent show

Have a talent show. Try to discover talents which other members of the church community are not aware of.

Reflecting

Use these ideas to help everyone to reflect and worship.

Who do you know?

Go round the group counting how many new names you know. (Be careful not to make anyone feel inadequate.)

Learning about each other

What new things have you learned about people? Ask people to say, 'I have discovered that...'

Labelling each other

Put a large label on the back of each person. Ask everyone to write on each label something positive about the person wearing it, for them to read at the end of the activity. (Do this in groups if there are too many of you.) Alternatively use a card or folded sheet of paper for each person.

Paper chain

Use strips of coloured sticky paper. Ask each person to write their name on their strip (help those who find this difficult). Join the strips together into a chain. Pray for everybody, by name if this is feasible.

Song

Sing a song or hymn about what individuals can offer to God, for example:

'If I were a butterfly' (*Junior Praise*, 94);

'I will bring to you' (*Come and Praise*, 59);

'Give me oil in my lamp' (*Come and Praise*, 43; *Junior Praise*, 50; *Hymns and Psalms*, 492; *Partners in Praise*, 5).

Reading

Read Psalm 139.1-10.

Prayer

> Lord,
> I may not have
> the great oratory of the preacher
> or the sensitive touches of a poet;
> I may not have
> the vision of an artist
> or the ear of a great musician,
> but I will strive to be
> all that I ought to be
> in your sight,
> and stretch my talents and skills
> to the uttermost
> so that your world is filled with beauty
> and my life becomes an offering of joy.

(By David Jenkins, reprinted from
The Word in the World, *NCEC, 1997)*

Going further

Has this session revealed interests and skills which people would like to explore further? Here are some ideas for doing this.

Sharing skills

What about finding new ways of developing and using your interests and skills? For example, you could draw up a skills register or set up a group to bring together people with a common interest.

Eating a meal

Bring the ingredients to make a light meal e.g. sandwiches or a ploughman's lunch.

Either:
Ask some people (of different ages) to prepare and eat their meal by themselves. Ask others to work in small groups, both for the preparation and for the eating of the meal. Bring the whole group together to share their feelings. Finish by eating a simple dessert all together.

Or:
Work in small groups to prepare the meal, then eat it all together.

Taking photographs

Take photographs of everybody in the life of the church. Either display them on a noticeboard or put them in an album. Add everybody's names and signatures. Don't display them in a hierarchy or in family groups; mix them up so that everyone can feel equally valued.

Finding me: Second session

Gathering

Bring everyone together for an opening act of worship.

Call to worship

> God is here.
> God is waiting for you and for me.
> Let us meet God together.

Hymn or song

'God who made the Earth' (*Come and Praise,* 10; *Rejoice and Sing*, 16);

'There are hundreds of sparrows' (*Come and Praise*, 15);

'When God made the garden of creation' (*Come and Praise,* 16);

'Life is great!' (see page 46).

Prayers of adoration and confession

Reading

Act out or read the story of Zacchaeus (Luke 19.1-10).

Doing and Reflecting

Either: all together in one place

Or: mixed-age groups in different parts of the building

All together in one place

Choose from these activities.

Who is this?
Do
Blindfold a small group of volunteers of different ages. Ask them to feel the face - nose, eyes, lips, hair - of one of their friends without telling them who it is. Can they guess who it is? How do they know?

Ask everyone to close their eyes. Get different people in turn to cough, laugh, sing or chuckle. Who can identify them?

Talkabout
✔ In what ways are we different from each other? How do we recognize each other?

✔ What is good about being different?

✔ Do some people get ignored, particularly if they are small, like children or Zacchaeus?

✔ Why was it significant that Jesus asked Zacchaeus if he could go to tea?

✔ What kinds of people do we choose to share meals with?

✔ What does this story tell us about God's attitude towards us?

Who am I?
Do
Give each person a piece of paper and a pencil or felt-tipped pen. Ask them to write their name in the middle of the paper and then to surround it with words or pictures to show their different roles in life, e.g. mother, daughter, sister, friend, housekeeper, accountant, church organist.

Talkabout
Ask people to talk about their roles in pairs or small groups.

✔ What do these roles reveal about you?

✔ How did Zacchaeus see his role? How do you think Jesus perceived it?

✔ How does Jesus view us?

Desert Island Discs

Do

Ask everybody to bring along four items that they would like to take with them if they were to be sent away to a desert island. In small groups, show your items and explain why they are important. (If it is not possible for everyone to do this, arrange for several people to participate and to share their items with the whole group.)

Talkabout

✓ What did the items reveal about the people who brought them?

✓ How did people feel about showing their items and talking about them?

✓ Why did Zacchaeus go to such lengths to see Jesus?

✓ Did Jesus put any pressure on him?

✓ What difference did it make to Zacchaeus that Jesus treated him as an individual rather than as just another member of the crowd?

✓ What difference does it make to you that Jesus treats us as individuals?

Mixed-age groups in different parts of the building

Choose as you feel appropriate.

Making our mark

Do

Provide thick powder paint in shallow trays and three large sheets of paper: one for handprints, one for fingerprints, one for footprints. You will also need an A4 sheet of paper for each person. Having protected clothes and surfaces, ask everyone to make their finger-, hand- and footprints on their own sheet of paper and on the large sheets.

Talkabout

Use a magnifying glass to look at the prints.

✓ What do you notice about the prints?

✓ Why is it useful that our prints are different? Does it matter that the differences are very small?

✓ What do these differences show us about God and how God thinks of us?

Small is clever?

Do

Provide some tasks which are better performed by people who are small: for example, getting through a small hoop, getting into a small space, retrieving an object from a small jar, finding things in awkward places.

Talkabout

✓ Think of some of the advantages of being small. How many examples can you find?

✓ What are the advantages of being tall?

✓ Was it an advantage to Zacchaeus to be small? What might have happened if he had been tall?

My secret file

Do

Tell the group that they have the opportunity to go by space shuttle to make contact with the life forms on a new planet. Before they leave they must prepare a secret file to give details about themselves. The file should contain self-portraits and other information (Suggestions may include: birthday, favourite colour, favourite item of clothing, name of best friend, hobby, etc). Provide paper, card, scissors, felt-tipped pens, sticky paper and glue.

Talkabout

✓ How does the information vary? Do the files tell everything?

✓ What kinds of things have been kept secret? Why?

✓ Are there some things we are embarrassed about and would not want others to know?

✓ Did Zacchaeus have things to be embarrassed about? What were they?

✓ How did Jesus feel about them? How did he make Zacchaeus feel?

✓ How does God behave towards us?

✓ What did Zacchaeus do to show Jesus how he felt about him?

✓ What can we do to show God how we feel?

What do I see?

Do

Give a copy of page 39 to each member of the group.

Ask people to fill the sections in, and then share their responses with someone else, if they wish to do so.

Talkabout

✓ What kinds of things do we recognize in ourselves?

✓ Why do we dislike some things about our-selves?

✓ What things might we want to change? What sorts of things must we learn to live with?

✓ What are the things we value in each other?

✓ Why did Jesus bother with Zacchaeus? What did he value in him? How did he show his regard?

✓ How do you think the people in the crowd felt? Do you think this incident changed their attitudes to Zacchaeus and to Jesus?

✓ What does the story say to you?

✓ What message does it have for people who feel that they are unpopular, despised or re-jected?

Concentric circles
(for older age-groups)

Do

Give each person a copy of page 40.

Working on your own, draw yourself or write your name in the central circle. In the next circle write the names of people whom you find it easiest to talk to. Work outwards, adding further names. Keep your diagram for personal reflection after-wards.

Talkabout

✓ How easy is it to share your private thoughts with somebody else?

✓ What would you tell a stranger about your-self?

✓ What would you tell a neighbour?

✓ What would you tell your parent?

✓ What would you tell your brother/sister/close relative?

✓ What would you tell your best friend?

✓ What would you tell God?

✓ Why are we sometimes more prepared to talk to a stranger than to one of our family?

✓ How much do we feel able to share with God?

✓ Jesus obviously knew all about Zacchaeus. How do we feel about God knowing all about us? To what extent do we try to hide from God?

✓ Are we as prepared for the call of God as Zacchaeus was?

Responding

Sharing

If you have been working in separate groups, come back together and share what you have been doing.

The Peace

Pass the Peace to the people around you.

Song

'Take this moment' (see page 44)

Prayers

We see ourselves, O God,
people of faith and faithlessness –
dancing in the sun one day
and overwhelmed by our realities on the next,
joyfully announcing the gospel sometimes
and then trembling in our uncertainty.
We see the hope that lies among us –
and hope that we could care
and live in community with each other
and the world.

(From Risking Obedience, *Prayer Handbook of the Uniting Church Australia)*

Joining in

Families share all kinds of things across the age-groups: talking to each other, reading stories, sharing meals, going out for the day. The church is one of the few places where there is the opportunity to meet people of different ages and to discover the fun of being together.

This part of *Count us in* will help you and your group to recognize that

✓   you are part of a Christian community within a wider community;

✓   you can learn from each other;

✓   a community can both exclude and include people;

✓   you can enjoy being together.

Using the story of the early Christian community, you will think about

✓   what it may have felt like to be part of that community;

✓   your experience of being part of the Christian community today.

The grid overleaf gives you an overview of the two sessions of *Joining in*. Detailed instructions are on the pages which follow.

Use the first session as an opportunity to enjoy being together as a church community of all ages and at all stages of Christian experience.

In the **Doing** part of the first session, make sure that you allow enough time to

✓   do activities in small groups;

✓   look at what the groups have done;

✓   share in a whole-group activity.

Use the second session as a framework for an act of worship. The activities suggested can also be used at another time.

Joining in: FIRST SESSION

Doing	Reflecting	Going Further
Mixed-age groups, choose from: Cooking Banner-making Stained-glass windows Group lego Wall collage News sheet User-friendly check on the premises Action group Badge-making **All together in one place, choose from:** Video Time line A tower What a surprise! Showing the video Graffiti wall Display Shared meal	**Choose from:** User-friendly check on the premises Time Capsule Web of community Song Reading Prayer	**Choose from:** Meals A day out Fun activities

Joining in: SECOND SESSION

Gathering	Doing and Reflecting	Responding
Call to worship Hymn or song Prayers Reading: Acts 2.42-47	**All together in one place** **Choose from:** Strength in numbers Where do we belong? Sharing our belongings What does it take? **Mixed-age groups** **Choose from:** Chime bars Friends Keep out! Someone new Jigsaw The 'in-crowd' What makes a healthy community?	Sharing Hymn or song Prayer Sharing the Peace

Joining in: First session

Doing

Activities to do in small groups

Use some of these ideas to help people of all ages to do things together.

Cooking

Choose a recipe for cakes or biscuits which is simple and suitable for people of all ages to make together. Make enough for the whole group to share later.

Banner-making

Design and make a banner, using one of these ideas or one of your own. Use pictures and patterns, not just words.

✓ Provide an old bed sheet which can be suspended from a broom handle. Cut templates out of paper and pin them to the fabric. Use aerosol cans of different coloured paints to spray the fabric. Remove the templates. (Protect the area with newspaper and, if possible, spray outdoors.)

✓ Make a collage using a large sheet of paper (e.g. from a flipchart) and a variety of materials (e.g. paper, fabric, pasta, sequins, feathers).

Stained-glass windows

Choose one of the following methods:

✓ Mark a pattern on white greaseproof paper with a pencil or dark felt-tipped pen. Fill in the design with coloured cellophane, tissue paper or watercolour paints.

✓ Draw a simple design on a sheet of black paper, using white chalk. Remember to leave black strips, representing leading between the different parts of the design. Cut out a section at a time, fastening tissue paper or cellophane of the appropriate colour to the back of the paper, to represent coloured glass.

Fix the completed 'window' to a clear glass window using sellotape or blu-tak.

Group lego

Provide a large quantity of 'lego' or 'duplo'. Let the group decide what to make and how to make it.

Wall collage

Fasten a very large sheet of paper to the wall. Provide scraps of fabric, coloured paper, newsprint, magazine pictures, felt-tipped pens and PVA adhesive. Encourage the group to make a picture or poster of their own choice.

News sheet

Make a news sheet or newspaper about your church. You might use a lap-top computer to prepare the text. Remember that some of the younger members of the group may have the greatest skill with computers.

A polaroid or digital camera may help with illustrations. Magazines and newspapers will give you ideas for layout and content.

User-friendly check on the premises

✓ What special needs do the users of your premises have? For example, do any people have difficulties with hearing, sight or mobility?

✓ What are the needs of the elderly and the very young?

✓ Do any parts of your premises present problems for these people or groups?

Discuss these questions with people who have to face these kinds of problems every time they come to your church. Find out what your church community could do to make things easier. If you are unable to talk to people themselves, try to simulate the experience of being in a wheelchair, being a small child, not being able to see clearly etc.

Report your findings not only to the whole group but also to whichever committee in your church is in a position to take action.

Action group

Identify and carry out a job that needs to be done on the church premises or in the nearby community, such as gardening or painting.

Badge-making

If you have, or can borrow, a badge-making machine, design and produce enough badges for everyone. Think of a symbol, logo or slogan for your church.

Video

Make a video (lasting about ten minutes) of everything that is going on in your church today.

Time line

Place a broad strip of paper along a wall. Mark the paper in sections representing the number of years that your present church, or an earlier building, has served your community. Show, in pictures, photographs, drawings or writing, major events in the life of your church.

A tower

Make a tower using only newspaper and sellotape. Try to make it as high as possible

What a surprise!

Make a structure from art straws which is strong enough to hold a brick.

Ideas for the whole group

Having shared in small groups, make sure that everyone has a chance to see what each group has done. Use one or more of the following activities to involve everyone.

Showing the video

Let everyone watch the video made by the small group.

Graffiti wall

Cover a wall with paper and ask everyone to draw a picture of themselves or make some mark or design to represent themselves.

Display

Ask everyone to share in making a display about your church and what it does. Use recent photographs of events, notices, newsletters and information on all the age-groups that meet on the premises. Include flags, artefacts and badges. Don't forget other groups who meet on your church premises.

Shared meal

Have a meal together, including any food prepared by a small group.

Reflecting

Use these ideas to help everyone to reflect and worship.

User-friendly check on the premises

Ask the small group to report back on their findings. Decide what action needs to be taken and by whom.

Time capsule

Divide everyone into small groups. Give each group a cardboard box in which to collect ten items which would tell someone 100 years from now about your church community of today.

Web of community

Use a ball of string to build up a web of community. Stand or sit in a circle. Hold onto the end of the string and throw the ball to another member of the group. As you do so, mention something you both have in common: e.g. 'We both have brown hair' or 'We both play table tennis'. Continue in this way, making sure that everyone is included in the web.

Song

'Bind us together' (*Junior Praise*, 17)

Reading

Romans 12.3-5, followed by:

Contact

Reach out my hand to touch
My neighbour, friend,
Or kith and kin.

Not quite;
Not far enough;
The gap's too great.
So I must lean,
Further and further,
Hand stretching out to hand.

What if I fall;
Lose balance and
       Upset
My equilibrium?

Perhaps I shall have to change my ground.

(By Donald Hilton, reprinted from
Flowing Streams, *NCEC, 1993)*

Prayer

May our church exist for others as it does
for ourselves.

May we work as hard for others as we do for
ourselves.

May we care as much about others as we do
about ourselves.

May we use our gifts as creatively for others
as we do for ourselves.

Take the life of your church, our work, our
care and our gifts
and use us to serve others in your name.

(By Simon Oxley, reprinted from
The Word in the World, *NCEC, 1997)*

Going Further

Meals

Share a meal either on or off the premises. Think about ways of making it different from anything you have done before: perhaps a picnic, a breakfast, a barbecue, or a safari meal where you eat each course at a different house.

A day out

Have a day out together. Make it a coach trip, a car treasure hunt, a visit to a local museum or a church walk.

Fun activities

Organize a concert, an all-age quiz, a craft afternoon, a barn dance, a local treasure hunt or other activity appropriate to your group and your situation.

Joining in: Second session

Gathering

Bring everyone together for an opening act of worship.

Call to worship

> God is here.
> God is waiting for us all.
> Let us meet God together.

Hymn or song

'God is here!' (*Hymns and Psalms*, 653; *Partners in Praise*, 127);

'Join with us' (*Come and Praise*, 30).

Prayers of adoration and confession

Reading

Read the story of the early Christian community (Acts 2.42-47).

This can be read by a group of three people of different ages taking two verses each.

Doing and Reflecting

Either: all together in one place

Or: mixed-age groups in different parts of the building

All together in one place

Choose from these activities.

Strength in numbers

Either:
Provide a small pile of thin sticks or twigs. Ask someone to break one. (It is hoped that they will be able to do so easily.) Tie the others into a bundle. Ask people to try to break the bundle in half. (The object is not to be able to do so!)

And/or:
Ask someone to tear in half a sheet of paper removed from an old telephone directory. Then ask them to tear the whole directory in half. (Some people may be interested in trying to see how many pages they can tear at one time before the task becomes impossible. Try to avoid a competition.)

And/or:
Choose a well-known song or hymn. Ask for volunteers to sing a solo. Ask for further volunteers to sing as a group. (It is hoped that more people will volunteer for the group.)

And/or:
Hold a quiz with a difference. Have one member in Team A and six in Team B. Which team does better?

Talkabout
- ✓ What was the point of the activity/activities you have just done?
- ✓ What difference does it make when a group works together?
- ✓ Share examples from your own experience of a group bringing about change: e.g. stopping the building of a bypass, changing a school rule.
- ✓ What benefit was it to the early church community for them to share so much together?
- ✓ How can you strengthen your community by working together?

Where do we belong?

Do
Have a selection of hats (real or toy) which belong to different categories or groups: e.g. police helmet, Brownie hat. Encourage people to try them on.

Talkabout
- ✓ To what groups do the wearers of the hats belong?
- ✓ What groups do you belong to? Make a list on a flipchart.
- ✓ What are the advantages/disadvantages of belonging to a group?

✓ What responsibilities are involved in belonging to a group?

✓ What were the advantages/disadvantages of belonging to the early Christian community?

✓ What are the advantages/disadvantages of belonging to your church?

Sharing our belongings

Do

Invite everyone to exchange (temporarily!) an item they are wearing (e.g. scarf, jumper, watch) with someone sitting nearby, and talk to each other. Hand the items back.

Talkabout

✓ How did you feel about being asked to share?

✓ What are the problems of sharing with other people?

✓ What problems do you think the early Christian community faced when they decided to share everything?

✓ What things ought you to learn to share within your church and wider community?

What does it take?

Break into smaller groups (at least two). Give one of the following questions to each group:

✓ What do you have to be like to be a follower of Jesus?

✓ What do you have to be like to be a member of this church?

Record your answers. Compare the findings of the groups.

Talkabout

✓ What have you learned about your church community?

✓ Do you think the people in the early church saw any difference between following Jesus and belonging to the Christian community?

✓ What are the implications of this exercise for your church?

Mixed-age groups in different parts of the building

Choose as you feel appropriate.

Chime bars

Do

Provide chime bars G A B C D and beaters. Ask a volunteer to play a tune on one chime bar. Ask four more to join in, each playing repeatedly on one chime bar. Then ask the group to work together, playing G B and D simultaneously followed by A and C simultaneously and then repeating this pattern several times.

Talkabout

✓ What was the point of the activity you have just done?

✓ What difference does it make when a group works together?

✓ What effect do you think the early church community had on those around them?

✓ What effect does your church community have on those around you?

Friends

Do

Give out large sheets of paper and thick felt-tipped pens or crayons. Ask people to draw themselves in the centre of their sheet of paper surrounded by pictures of their family and friends.

Talkabout

✓ Who are the people in the pictures?

✓ What do you like doing with them?

✓ What can you do better with your friends?

✓ Are there things you particularly like doing with your friends in the church?

Keep out!

Do

Form a circle holding hands, leaving several people out. They must try to break into the circle while those holding hands try to stop them. They may only use their arms and bodies and must not let go of hands. When those who were outside the circle have been successful, swap over to give other people a go.

Talkabout

✓ What did it feel like to be excluded?

✓ How did it feel to break into the group?

✓ How did it feel to shut others out?

✓ What did you feel when others broke into the group?

✓ In what real-life situations have you felt the same?

✓ What does this say to you about the church?

Someone new

Do

Imagine that a new person wants to join your group. Ask an established, confident member of the group to act out the part of the newcomer. Without any words, show that the newcomer is not wanted.

Now devise a drama on making a newcomer welcome (showing them round, letting them join in etc). Draw up a list of suggestions to make them feel at home.

Talkabout

✓ Share experiences of being a newcomer.

✓ How do you make people feel welcome in your church?

Jigsaw

Do

Have ready a large picture glued onto thin card. Cut it into 'jigsaw' pieces, making sure that there are enough for all members of the group. Mix the pieces up and distribute them, but keep some back. Build up the picture.

Talkabout

✓ How does it feel not to be able to complete the picture?

✓ Have you experienced an equivalent situation in real life?

Do

Complete the picture using the pieces which you kept back.

Talkabout

✓ How do you feel now that you can see the whole picture?

✓ Do you think that members of the early Christian community thought that they could see 'the whole picture'?

✓ How did this affect their lifestyle?

✓ How much of 'the picture' can you see?

✓ How should your perspective affect your lifestyle?

The 'in-crowd'

Do

Divide into three groups. Ask each group to find something that they all have in common: e.g. all born in a hospital or all wearing red socks. Each group takes it in turn to be questioned by the others in order that they can identify the characteristic and discover which of them is also part of the 'in-crowd'. Questions may only be answered by 'yes', 'no' or 'don't know'.

Talkabout

✓ How does it feel to be part of the 'in-crowd'?

✓ How does it feel to be excluded?

✓ Is there an 'in-crowd' in your church? If so, do you feel part of it?

✓ Are all Christians part of the 'in-crowd'?

What makes a healthy community?
(for older age-groups)

Use copies of page 41.

✓ How healthy is your church community?

✓ Where is it succeeding?

✓ Where is it failing?

✓ Draw up a fitness regime for your church.

Responding

Sharing

If you have been working in separate groups, come back together and share what you have been doing.

Song

'Brother, sister, let me serve you' (see page 47);

'As your family, Lord' (*Hymns and Psalms*, 595).

Prayer

Lord Jesus Christ,
we pray that we
who are amongst those
who most frequently mention your name
may also be found amongst those
who most urgently seek your truth,
most deeply explore your ways
and most readily live in your resurrection
light.

*(By Donald Hilton, reprinted from
The Word in the World, NCEC, 1997)*

Sharing the Peace

Sing 'Halle, halle, halle' (see page 45) as you share the Peace in African style. To do this the leader of the group opens the door and stands beside it. Someone shares the Peace with the leader and then stands beside and beyond the leader, beginning a chain which will snake out into the corridor/vestibule/open air. Continue in this way until everyone has had the chance to share the Peace with each other.

We're in it together, God

The experience of being a community of all ages is an important part of what we bring to worship. Through our diversity we bring a richness and variety of insights which it is right to reflect and celebrate. We belong not just to the church but to each other.

This part of *Count us in* will help you and your group to explore

✓ how worship arises out of shared experience;

✓ what people of all ages can contribute to worship;

✓ the value of active participation in worship.

Using the story of the feeding of the five thousand, you will recognize that:

✓ worship is enriched by the use of all your senses;

✓ God needs everyone to play their part;

✓ allowing space for God to act involves risk.

The grid overleaf gives you an overview of *We're in it together, God*. Detailed instructions are on the pages which follow.

Use *We're in it together, God* to help you to share in the experience of preparing and joining in worship. A Sunday morning may be the best time in which to explore this together.

Begin with **Gathering**, meeting all together for worship. Follow this with **Doing** - go into groups for 30 minutes to work together on different aspects of the theme. (You will need at least one person to be responsible for each separate activity.) Finally, come back together for **Reflecting** and **Responding**, for which an outline is given but you may prefer to do things your own way.

We're in it together, God

Gathering	Doing	Reflecting and responding
Call to worship Hymn or song Prayers Reading: John 6.1-13	**Mixed-age groups:** Telling the story Preparing the loaves Making fish Setting up a worship centre Creating prayers of intercession Preparing music	**All together in one place:** Song Telling the story Offering of the loaves Reflection Offering of the fish Song Sharing of the loaves Prayers of intercesison Song Distribution of the fish Prayers Song Blessing

Gathering

Bring everyone together for an opening act of worship.

Call to worship

> God is here.
> God is waiting for us all.
> Let us worship God together.

Hymn or song

'There's a spirit in the air' (*Hymns and Psalms*, 326; *Rejoice and Sing*, 329; *Partners in Praise*, 125)

Prayer

> Lord, as we worship today give us vision.
> Move us by your Spirit.
> Bring good news to us all,
> freedom to broken people,
> and Heaven, here on Earth.
>
> Open our eyes to see you as you really are,
> and open our hearts to praise you.
> Give us a vision that will carry us through
> our disappointments and our failures,
> our anxious and unhappy times,
> and the monotony of boring routines.
>
> Give us a vision that will lift our lives
> and lead us to new ways of service.
>
> Help us to dare to dream of love
> in a world that speaks of hate
> Help us to dare to dream of peace
> in a world that speaks of war.
>
> In our worship today, Lord, give us vision
> through Jesus Christ our Lord.

(From the MAYC London Weekend Worship)

Reading

Read, or ask a good story-teller to tell, the story of the feeding of the five thousand (John 6.1-13).

Doing

Mixed-age groups in different parts of the building

Spend 30 minutes in these groups working on different aspects of the theme.

Telling the story

Prepare to act out the story or mime it while it is read. Create characters, costumes and props as you wish.

Preparing the loaves

Either: cook part-baked rolls.

Or: make and cook rolls using dough prepared in advance.

You will also need to have ready baskets to put the rolls in.

Making fish

You will need to have one paper fish for each person taking part in *We're in it together, God.*

Either: prepare the fish shapes in advance and provide glitter sticks, sequins, glue etc. for decoration.

Or: if numbers and time permit, prepare and decorate the fish in the group.

Setting up a worship centre

At the front of the worship area, create a worship centre using low tables, the chancel steps or cardboard boxes. Cover with drapes. Place a wicker picnic hamper or large basket on the worship centre, leaving space for a basket of rolls. Gather on and around the worship centre things which have been made, written or used during *Count us in*.

Creating prayers of intercession

Think of people for whom you want to pray:

✓   in your church community;

✓   in your local community;

✓   in the news today.

Use your church magazine, local newspapers etc. Prepare prayers, including a response in which everyone can join.

Preparing music

Choose one or two hymns or songs on the theme of being part of a community and the contribution that individuals can make. As a group, rehearse the song 'Caring, sharing' (see page 48). You will need someone to be precentor while the others respond. Also choose a piece of quiet music to be played (either live or on CD or tape) during the offering of the fish.

Reflecting and Responding

All together in one place - suggested outline

As people come back together, the members of the 'fish group' give each person a fish and ask them to write their name on it.

Song

Sing one of the songs chosen by the music group.

Telling the story

The group re-enacts the story of the feeding of the five thousand.

Offering of the loaves

Members of the loaf-making group bring forward the baskets of rolls and place them beside the hamper on the worship centre.

Reflection

Talkabout

How do you think the boy in the story must have felt? When have you felt the same? Share your thoughts with people near you.

Thinkabout

What do you have to offer – to God, to your church, to the community? Is there something new you wish to offer in the light of your experience of *Count us in*?

Offering of the fish

Bring your fish forward and place it in the hamper on the worship centre as a sign of offering yourself to God. (If anyone is unable to do this, they can hand their fish to someone else to take it forward for them.) Play quiet music while this is going on.

Song

Sing a song or hymn of commitment.

Sharing of the loaves

Share the rolls as a sign of God's self-offering to us.

Distribute some of the rolls at random. Ask people to break them in half, giving one half away. Continue to do this until everyone has a piece of bread.

Read John 6.11. Eat the bread.

Prayers of intercession

Members of the prayer group lead the intercessions.

Song

Sing 'Caring, sharing' (see page 48), asking everyone to join in the 'echoes'.

Distribution of the fish

Members of the 'fish group' collect handfuls of the fish and distribute them, while 'Caring, sharing' is played quietly in the background.

Prayers

Pray silently for the person whose name is on the fish you have received.

Close the time of prayer with these words:

> Loving God, thank you for loving us even though we are all different.

> Living God, thank you for living amongst us and reaching out to others through us.

Song

Either: sing one or more verses of 'Caring, sharing' again.

Or: sing a song or hymn of your choice.

Blessing

Stand up and be counted

This is the final part of *Count us in*. It gives suggestions for preparing worship and for celebrating together. You will find ideas for developing an act of worship to mark the end of *Count us in* and the beginning of a new stage of the life of your church community.

You may want to choose your own theme and develop it in your own way, particularly if you are celebrating at a specific time of year, such as Advent. You may want to base your service on worship and learning materials such as *Partners in Learning*. You may want to take the parable of the lost son (Luke 15.11-32) as your starting point, using the suggestions given on pages 35-36. Whatever you do, try to involve as many people as possible.

You will find it helpful to plan a preparation day or half-day, perhaps on the Saturday before worshipping on the Sunday. Alternatively you might plan to have Sunday lunch together, prepare during the afternoon and worship in the early evening. Other options are possible; choose whichever suits your situation best.

This part of *Count us in* will help you and your group to:

✓   involve people of all ages, abilities, gifts and needs;

✓   prepare worship;

✓   worship together, using the ideas and materials that they have suggested and prepared;

✓   realize that everyone has something to bring to worship.

Getting ready for the preparation day

✓ Form a small planning group. Arrange to meet well before the main preparation day.

✓ Have a broad idea of a possible approach in advance, but do not prepare so much that you will stifle people's ideas.

✓ Decide what groups you will need to prepare the act of worship (see the suggestions below).

✓ Choose 'enablers' for the groups. Encourage them to think as broadly as possible about what their group might need and to provide materials to cover a wide range of possibilities. Musicians, in particular, need a good variety of music and perhaps some percussion instruments. Those preparing for craft groups or for a young children's group also need to think very carefully about the materials they may need.

✓ Plan the practical details of the day, e.g. premises, refreshments.

✓ Make sure that a facilitator is available to 'pull everything together' - it can get a little exciting at the last moment - and to be a source of calm and reassurance.

✓ If possible, have a photocopier available, and/or an overhead projector with acetates.

Preparation day

✓ Begin with a short act of worship linked to the theme. Not only is it good to worship together but it starts people thinking. If possible, sit in a circle focusing on a worship centre.

✓ Give a brief explanation of the task and allow people, perhaps with a little gentle persuasion, to choose which group they will join. It is likely that everyone will feel insecure at this point and need reassurance.

✓ Work in groups, providing the opportunity for people to help themselves to drinks when appropriate.

✓ The facilitator should make sure that the groups liaise with each other (e.g. if the prayer group suggests a Taizé response to be sung during the intercessions, it needs to consult the music group).

✓ Have a meal together. It is helpful if this does not take too much preparation unless there are volunteers who see this as their main task. If not, consider ordering fish and chips from a local shop - if you have one.

✓ End with a short act of worship. If possible, allow time for people to reflect on what they have done in their groups. (If you are preparing on the same day as the main act of worship, however, you may want to finish with a prayer at this point.)

Before the act of worship

✓ If possible, give each participant an order of service so that they know when it is time for their contribution.

✓ Get to church in very good time for the service. When people are taking part they almost invariably come early and need encouragement that all is well.

Suggested groups

Groups preparing the act of worship should have people of all ages in them (though you may prefer to have a special group for the under-fives). Choose groups which are appropriate to your situation and the theme.

The context of worship

Create a worship centre to link with the theme. Look at different ways of using the worship area imaginatively, e.g. the layout of seating, the use of windowsills, the creation of an area for drama.

Ministry of the Word

Choose a starting point. This might be the biblical material, the theme or your local context. In one or more groups, explore it using dramatized reading, mime, dance or drama.

Music

Find hymns, songs, and other music to link with the theme. Write new words to a familiar tune, work out a percussion accompaniment to a song or hymn, learn a new hymn to perform or to teach to others.

Prayer

Write or find prayers for different stages of the act of worship. These might include: thanksgiving, confession, intercession. Try to find ways of including everyone e.g. by using spoken or sung responses.

Making links

Explore the theme in the context of your neighbourhood, town, country and the world.

Creative arts

Make banners, arrange flowers, decorate the church etc.

Under-fives

If you feel it appropriate, plan separate activities for young children, linked to the theme. Remember to include them in the worship too.

✓ Have other groups as appropriate.

Ideas for an act of worship based on the parable of the lost son

Luke 15.11-32

Look at this parable in the context of all that you have experienced while working on *Count us in*. Consider the three main characters. To what extent did each of them feel accepted, affirmed, counted in? Begin to explore these questions and others, both in the planning group and in the different task groups which prepare for the main act of worship.

Opening worship for planning session

Create a worship centre using drapes in two different colours. One side (A) will represent exclusion and rejection, the other (B) will represent inclusion and acceptance. On side A place pea pods/bean husks and crusts of dry bread. On side B place a cake with candles on it.

Spend a few moments reflecting on experiences of rejection and of inclusion, using the parable and the worship centre.

Task groups

The context of worship

Recreate the worship centre at a focal point in the church. To side A add further symbols and pictures of rejection and exclusion. To side B add further symbols and pictures of acceptance and inclusion, including things to do with parties e.g. an invitation and food.

Decorate side B of the church with balloons, banners, streamers etc. to give a party atmosphere. Keep side A as bare as possible.

Ministry of the Word

Decide on a way (or ways) of presenting the parable through drama, liturgical dance, mime or dramatic reading.

Liaise with the 'context of worship' group. Find ways of using what they have done to help the congregation to think about these questions:

✓ What does it feel like to be sitting on the decorated side of the church?

✓ What does it feel like to be sitting on the bare side of the church?

Ask people to change sides. How do they feel now?

If you wish, use the imaginary letter on page 42 as a reading or as the basis of a dialogue.

Music

As part of the group's work, consider using one or both of the hymns on pages 44 and 47.

Prayer

Think about the three main characters in the parable. If they had written prayers of confession, what do you think they would have said? How does this link with your own experience? Make up prayers of confession to reflect this.

Do the same on the theme of forgiveness.

Making links

Explore ways in which your church can play a greater part in your local community and ways in which groups within the local community can be more involved in the life of the church. How will you present your ideas in the act of worship?

Creative arts

Make banners, streamers, flower arrangements etc. to decorate side B of the church. Liaise with the 'context of worship' group.

Hospitality

Help people to feel at home, as they arrive for the act of worship and at the celebration party afterwards. Prepare party food, e.g. jellies. Make *Count us in* cards (see page 43) - enough to give to everyone in the act of worship.

Under-fives

Make simple party food. Decorate balloons using felt-tipped pens. Learn to sing 'Caring, sharing' (see page 48). Talk about the story of the lost son.

Planning the act of worship

Use the contributions of the groups to create the act of worship. Towards the end of the service, arrange that the party decorations will be spread around the whole church or that extra ones will be brought in. When this has been done, ask the 'hospitality' group to give out the *Count us in* cards. Stand to sing 'Halle, Halle, Halle' (see page 46).

After the service, have a party to celebrate the end of *Count us in* and the start of the next phase of your church's life.

What next?

Now you have done Count us in, what next?

Here are some suggestions:

✓ Talk about your experiences in different groups within the life of the church. How did it feel to worship God all together? What was good? What was not so good?

✓ Try preparing more worship together e.g. for a festival.

✓ Meet together regularly as a church community, with all ages sharing in the next steps.

✓ Continue to plan all-age experiences, meals and outings.

✓ Remember to support activities in the community in which you live.

✓ Look at your church magazine. Is it all-age, both in contributions and in leadership?

✓ Ask yourselves at regular intervals, 'Are we doing things differently?'

Over to you... !

Questionnaire

Who is wearing green socks?	Who has been on an aeroplane in the last year?	Who has a birthday this month?
Who has done a reading in church?	Who has been given a certificate in the last year?	Who went shopping yesterday?
Who has had their hair cut in the last two weeks?	Who is wearing a T-shirt with a picture on it?	Who has visited someone who is ill in the last year?
Who plays a musical instrument?	Who has helped to take up the offering in church in the last month?	Who has seen their grandparent or grandchild in the last week?

What do I see?

What do I like about myself?	What would I like to change about me?	How do I think other people see me?

Concentric Circles

Traits of a healthy community

1   The members of a healthy community communicate and listen.

2   The members of a healthy community affirm and support one another.

3   The healthy community teaches respect for others.

4   The healthy community develops a sense of trust.

5   The healthy community has a sense of play and humour.

6   The healthy community exhibits a sense of shared responsibility.

7   The healthy community teaches a sense of right and wrong.

8   The healthy community has a strong sense of community in which rituals and traditions abound.

9   The healthy community has a balance of interaction amongst members.

10 The healthy community has a shared religious core.

11 The healthy community respects privacy.

12 The healthy community values service to others.

(From *Spectrum* youth work training course,

first edition, NCEC 1989)

Letter to an erstwhile prodigal son (by Geoffrey King)

Dear John,

You'll probably be most surprised to receive this letter from me, but I thought it the best way - to put things down on papyrus and let you know how my mind's been working, as it's some months since your return and although we work together we don't talk much again yet, do we? But I've had hours of counselling from our saintly, all-loving father and he has helped me to see things very differently since that morning I just walked away from you both in absolute disgust. More about those talks later.

First of all, I address you as 'John'. I know we're closely related but I just can't seem to bring myself to use that special word – but honestly, I am working on it; well, on myself, I really mean.

I don't suppose Dad has really put his side of the story, let alone mine, so I think it's only fair that I should put some things straight and get them off my chest at the outset. To start with, has he told you what a struggle we had to raise the money to buy out your share of the property before you went? You gave hardly any notice and no one can raise that amount of cash overnight. Some of the property had to be sold on the open market so that we could keep the farm and the livestock after the high valuation put on it all. And that meant the rents were down considerably. We also had to make some workers redundant which meant all of us working harder. However, with hard slogging from us all (while you were having a high old time for quite a while, I guess), we've managed to buy it all back.

As for our dear old Dad, he worked like the proverbial Trojan long after he should have retired, maybe so that I wouldn't suffer even more, but I suspect also to ensure you will still have a good inheritance again when he eventually shuffles off this mortal coil. No, it's all right. Now I can live with the thought of you inheriting again, which shows I've travelled a considerable way in my fight against bitterness, doesn't it? You never know, at this rate I may be able to use that special word before the end of this letter. I do accept that you latterly had a pretty miserable time when your money had run out, before you came to your senses. I'm really quite grateful to those pigs for letting you share their husks or whatever it was in their troughs. I must admit that part of the story has helped me a lot in my fight with myself! Also, I've not known what it was like to have so-called friends who didn't want to know you when you were down on your uppers.

But you've no idea how Dad was, very soon after you'd gone away to foreign parts, wherever they were. You've not told me yet. He grieved for you from the start, but then he was always sure you'd come back sooner or later. He'd go up to our highest field every morning before starting work to scan the horizon, and that's how he saw you from afar. I don't know why, but he was sure you'd come back early in the morning, having spent another rough night in a hedgerow after your money was through. He wanted to buy one of those marvellous instruments that lets you look at the stars. As it was, we only managed to stop him building a tower to see further by reminding him of the wicked Tower of Babel with which we suggested people might confuse it.

I can see now, though, after much working through, that it must have been terribly hard for him toiling alongside me, the rather serious one, thinking of the fun times he used to have with you, his younger and, let's face it, favourite son. No, don't worry; I'm not nearly as bitter as I was. I can see much clearer now and it's certainly helped a great deal writing these thoughts down. Dad was quite right – as usual. In fact, I'm nearly ready to use that word.

Another thing that's helping me is that Dad is insisting I throw a party for my friends. He says he's always got more than one fatted calf, anyway! I've got to admit, I've been so mad with you while you've been away that I've very much neglected my pals. So here is the ultimate shaft of my letter – the goal to which I've been striving: I'm having a dinner in three weeks' time, and the chief guests are to be my father and you, my BROTHER.

Yours in anticipatory, healing tears,

Christopher

My hope for God's world:

Someone I can help:

Something I can do:

....
(signed)

Please God,
(Count me in ✓)

Count us in

Music

Take this Moment

The Iona Community

Take this mo-ment, sign and space; Take my friends a - round;

Here a - mong us make the place Where your love is found.

2. Take the time to call my name,
   Take the time to mend.
   Who I am and what I've been,
   All I've failed to tend.

3. Take the tiredness of my days,
   Take my past regret,
   Letting your forgiveness touch
   All I can't forget.

4. Take the little child in me,
   Scared of growing old;
   Help him/her here to find his/her worth
   Made in Christ's own mould.

5. Take my talents, take my skills,
   Take what's yet to be;
   Let my life be yours, and yet,
   Let it still be me.

The Iona Community

Music

Halle, Hallelujah!

Caribbean arr. Geoff Weaver

traditional

45

Music

Life is Great

Peter Cutts (1937–)

Life is great! So sing a-bout it, As we can and as we should —

Shops and bus - es, towns and peo - ple, Vil - lage, farm - land, field and wood.

Life is great and life is giv - en, Life is love - ly, free and good.

2. Life is great!—whatever happens,
Snow or sunshine, joy or pain,
Hardship, grief or disillusion,
Suffering that I can't explain—
Life is great if someone loves me,
Holds my hand and calls my name.

3. Love is great!—the love of lovers,
Whispered words and longing eyes;
Love that gazes at the cradle
Where a child of loving lies;
Love that lasts when youth has faded,
Bends with age, but never dies.

4. Love is giving and receiving
Boy and girl, or friend and friend,
Love is hearing and forgiving
All the hurts that hate can send.
Love's the greatest way of living,
Hoping, trusting to the end.

5. God is great! In Christ he loved us,
As we should but never can—
Love that suffered, hoped and trusted
When disciples turned and ran,
Love that broke through death for ever.
Praise that loving, living Man!

Brian A. Wren (1936–)

Music

Servant Song

Richard Gillard (1953–)
arr. Betty Pulkingham (1928–)

Bro - ther, Sis - ter, let me serve you, Let me be as Christ to you;

Pray that I may have the grace to Let you be my ser - vant too.

2. We are pilgrims on a journey,
And companions on the road;
We are here to help each other
Walk the mile and bear the load.

3. I will hold the Christ-light for you
In the night-time of your fear;
I will hold my hand out to you,
Speak the peace you long to hear.

4. I will weep when you are weeping;
When you laugh I'll laugh with you;
I will share your joy and sorrow
Till we've seen this journey through.

5. When we sing to God in heaven
We shall find such harmony,
Born of all we've known together
Of Christ's love and agony.

6. Brother, Sister, let me serve you,
Let me be as Christ to you;
Pray that I may have the grace to
Let you be my servant too.

Richard Gillard (1953–)

Music

Caring, Sharing

Linda Caroe (1952–)
arr. Jeanne Harper

Walking pace, cheerfully ♩ = 112

Leader: Car-ing, shar-ing, Lov-ing, giv-ing,
Echo: car-ing, shar-ing, lov-ing, giv-ing,

mf
All: Liv-ing the Je-sus way.

2. Seeing, (seeing), helping, (helping),
   Loving, (loving), trusting, (trusting),
   Living the Jesus way.

3. Praying, (praying), obeying, (obeying),
   Loving, (loving), forgiving, (forgiving),
   Living the Jesus way.

Linda Caroe (1952–)

This song can be sung by the leader with children echoing or by two groups of children, the older ones taking the lead. It is also suitable for all ages. Ask the children to suggest simple actions.